Mary Grace Rodarte

Ariel Books

**Andrews McMeel
Publishing**

Kansas City

ELVIS
The King of Rock 'n' Roll

Elvis: The King of Rock 'n' Roll copyright © 2004 by Armand Eisen. All rights reserved. Printed in China. No part of this book may be used or reproduced in any manner whatsoever without written permission except in the case of reprints in the context of reviews. For information write Andrews McMeel Publishing, an Andrews McMeel Universal company, 4520 Main Street, Kansas City, Missouri 64111.

Photographs by Photofest

ISBN: 0-7407-4726-6
Library of Congress Control Number: 2004102932

Introduction

There's nothing quite like the power of the individual, the attraction of someone who has the knack of being completely himself. Perhaps that's why people the world over so loved, and continue to love, Elvis Presley. When kids his age were wearing jeans and T-shirts, he was wearing dress pants and neckerchiefs. While his friends were outside playing games in the street, he was inside, singing gospel with the church choir. When an unknown country boy walked into a recording studio on a hot summer day in 1953 and was asked the now-famous question by the woman running the studio, "Who do you sound like?" he answered, in a defining moment, "I don't sound like nobody."

Elvis: The King of Rock 'n' Roll

Elvis Presley was an American original: He was larger than life but was still down-to-earth enough to claim fried peanut-butter-and-banana sandwiches as one of his favorite foods. He loved fame, but he loved his family and friends more. The press tried to pin him down with titles like the "male Monroe," the "atomic powered singer," "Elvis the Pelvis," and "the King," but Elvis, ultimately, was just . . . Elvis.

Before ELV

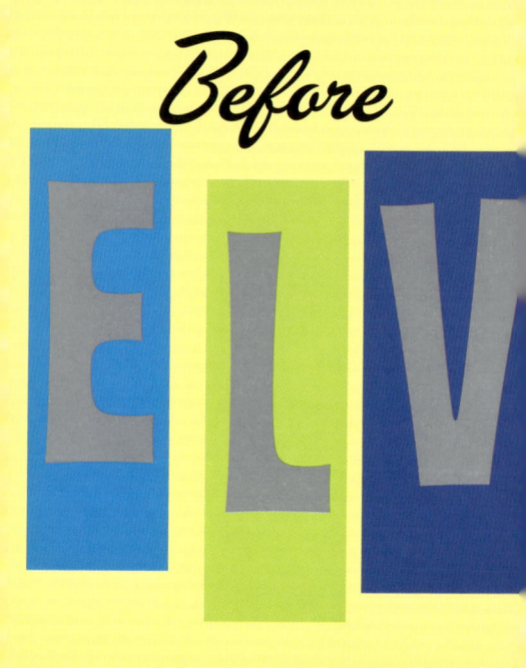

ELVIS PRESLEY

is the greatest
cultural force in
the twentieth
century.

—Leonard Bernstein,
composer and conductor

Folklore has it that the three most recognized words in the world are "Jesus," "Coca-Cola," and... *"Elvis."*

Life put out a "Millennium" issue of its magazine that listed the top one hundred events that have shaped world history: *Elvis Presley* singing rock 'n' roll came in at number ninety-nine.

Elvis: The King of Rock 'n' Roll

Some people tap their feet, some people snap their fingers, and some people sway back and forth. I just sorta do 'em all together, I guess.

—*Elvis Presley*

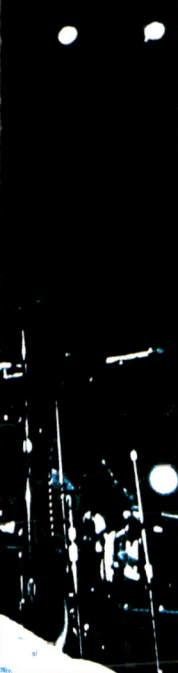

Spasms ran through both his legs, and soon the entire midsection of his body was jolting as if he'd swallowed a jackhammer.

—C. Robert Jennings, columnist for the *Saturday Evening Post*

When I feel depressed I just sit in my apartment and talk to *Elvis Presley*. He takes care of me. My house is covered with pictures of E L

Elvis: The King of Rock 'n' Roll

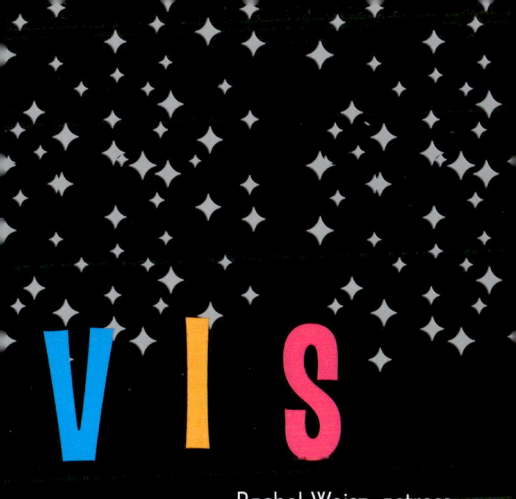

—Rachel Weisz, actress

An anagram is a word that is formed from rearranging the letters of an existing word. For example: Elvis lives!

Elvis: The King of Rock 'n' Roll

It's more **important** to try to surround yourself with people who can give you a little happiness, because you only pass through this life once, Jack. You don't come back for an encore.

—Elvis Presley

Elvis: The King of Rock 'n' Roll

More people visit **ELVIS'S** palatial estate, Graceland, than any other home except the White House.

E L V

Elvis failed his first semester of high school music theory class.

I S

It's said that the day Elvis died, every florist in Memphis ran out of flowers.

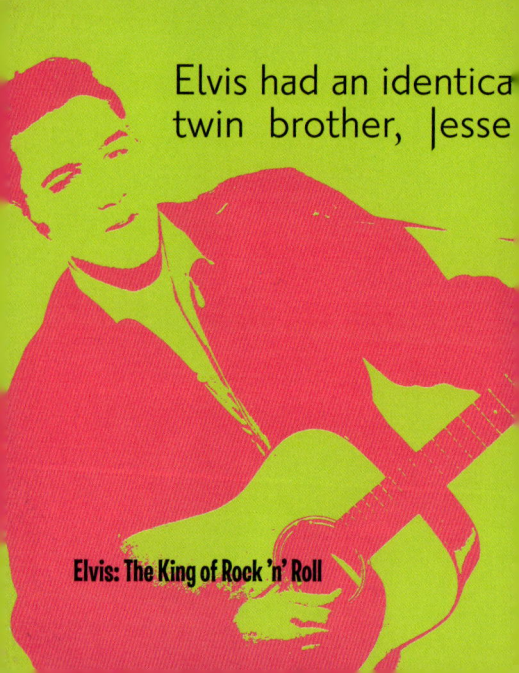

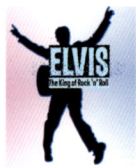

I don't know anything about music. In my line, you don't have to.

—Elvis Presley

Elvis: The King of Rock 'n' Roll

We were the only band in history that was directed by an ass.

—Scotty Moore, backup musician for Elvis, on the "Elvis the Pelvis" phenomenon

Historian David Halberstam wrote that the three most important events of the 1950s were the *Brown v. Board of Education* Supreme Court decision banning segregation in schools; the building of Levittown, a planned suburban community; and the arrival of *Elvis.*

Elvis: The King of Rock 'n' Roll

ELVIS

is the subject of more than 300 college courses.

Try to pass twenty-four hours in the United States without hearing

ELVIS PR

ESLEY'S

name or seeing his image. It's virtually impossible.

—*New York Times*, October 30, 1994

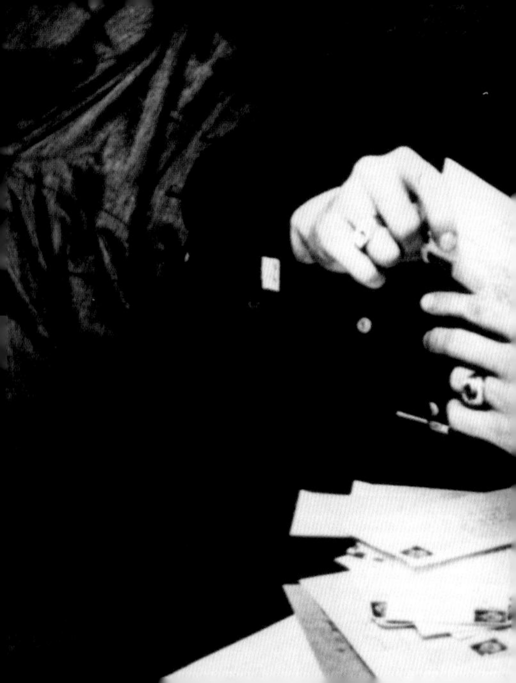

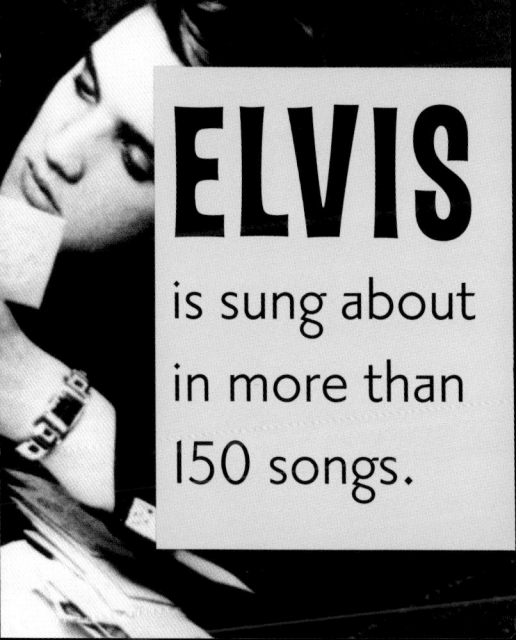

ELVIS

is sung about in more than 150 songs.

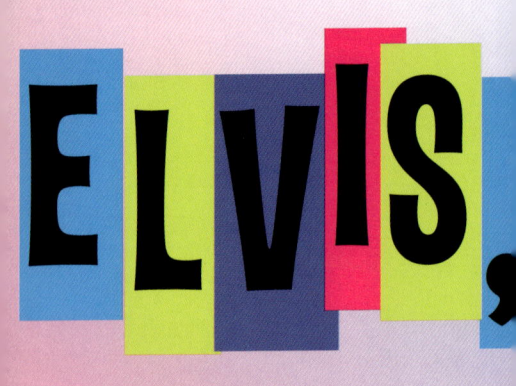

ELVIS,

Elvis: The King of Rock 'n' Roll

named after his father, Vernon Elvis Presley, was born in a two-room home in Tupelo, Mississippi, in 1935.

Elvis was very close to his mother, Gladys, who had many pet names for him. "Sat'nin" was one of her favorites.

Elvis: The King of Rock 'n' Roll

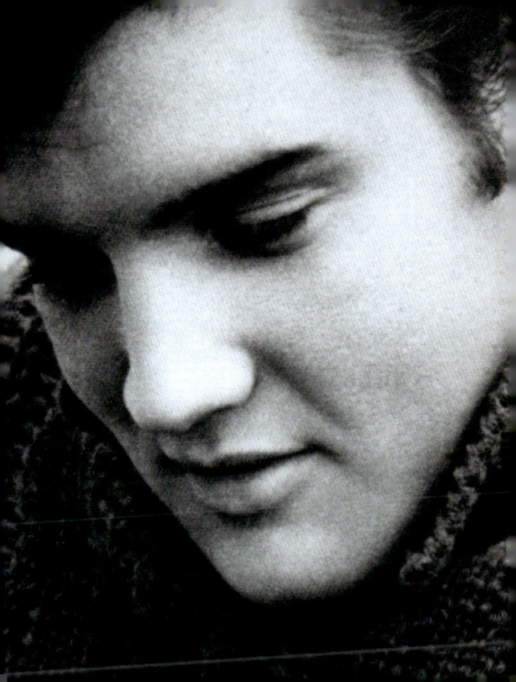

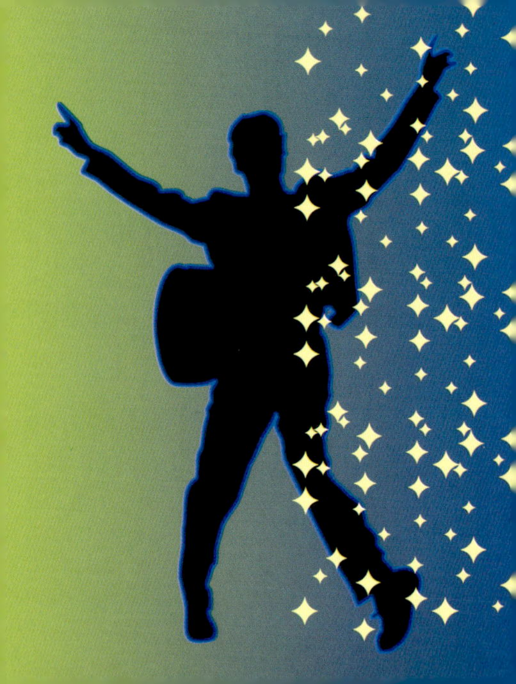

When *Elvis* was ten years old, he made his solo debut, singing in a talent contest at the annual Mississippi-Alabama Fair. He sang a tune called "Old Shep" and finished in fifth place.

ELV

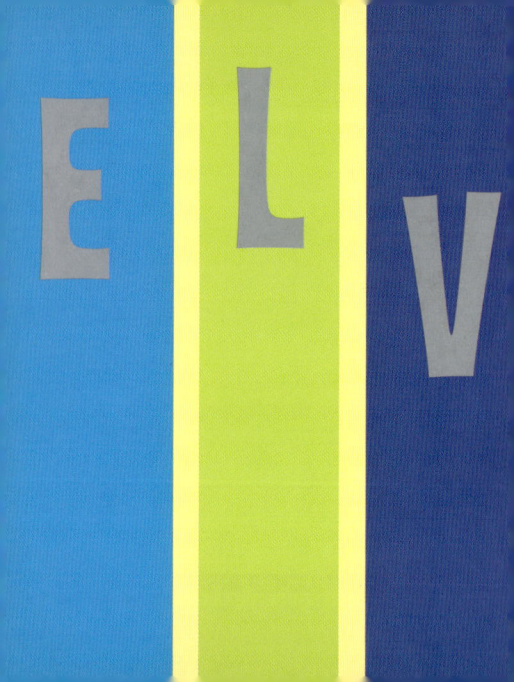

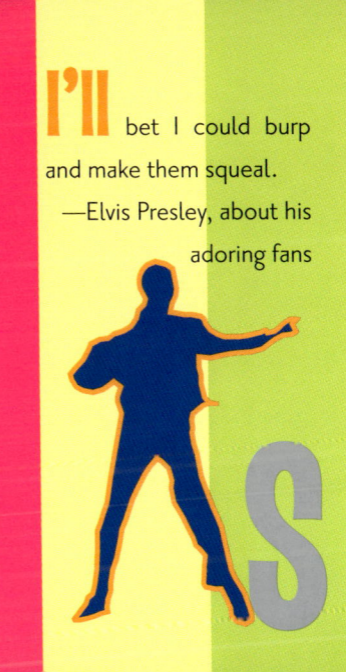

I'll bet I could burp and make them squeal.
—Elvis Presley, about his adoring fans

Elvis received his first guitar on the occasion of his eleventh birthday. He had originally asked for a rifle, but Gladys, his mother, refused to buy him a gun.

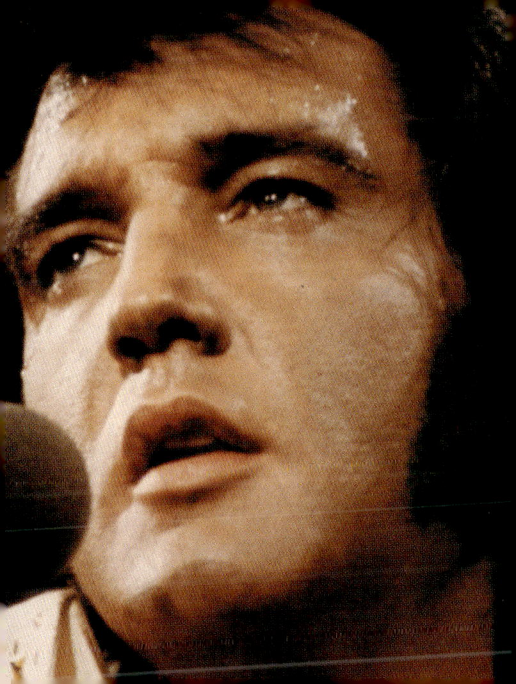

As a youth, *Elvis* preferred to wear dress pants rather than the jeans kids his age wore.

Elvis: The King of Rock 'n' Roll

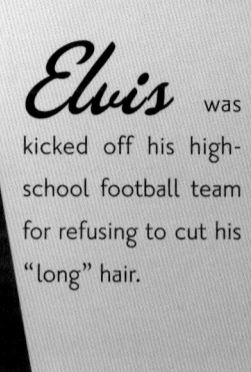

Elvis was kicked off his high-school football team for refusing to cut his "long" hair.

In the summer of 1953, an unheard-of Elvis Presley walked into the Memphis Recording Service to record two songs as a present for his mother's birthday. Sam Phillips, who owned the studio, was out to lunch and his assistant, Marion Keisker, was running the studio. She asked Elvis who he sounded like. "I don't sound like nobody," he answered.

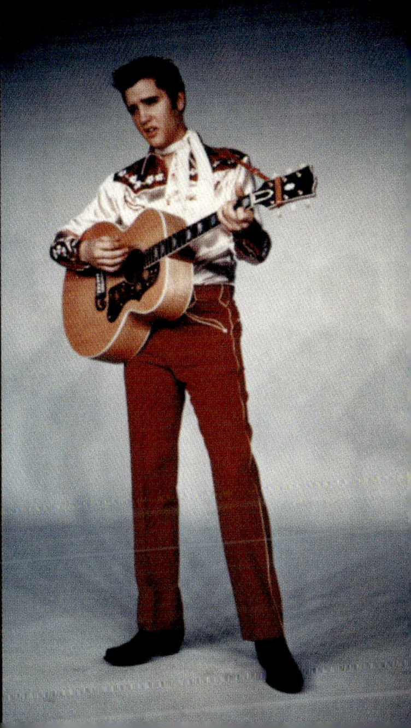

Music should be something that
something that

makes you gotta move, inside or outside.

—*Elvis Presley*

Elvis: The King of Rock 'n' Roll

IS

made his first appearance in front of a large audience at the outdoor Overton Park band shell in Memphis. He was billed in a newspaper ad as "Ellis Presley."

Memphis radio listeners heard *Elvis Presley* for the first time when his recording of "That's All Right" was played on the evening of July 8, 1954, at approximately 9:30 P.M.

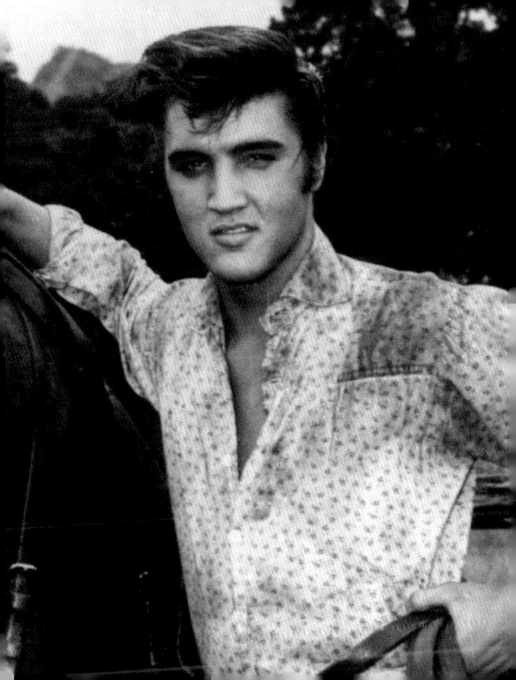

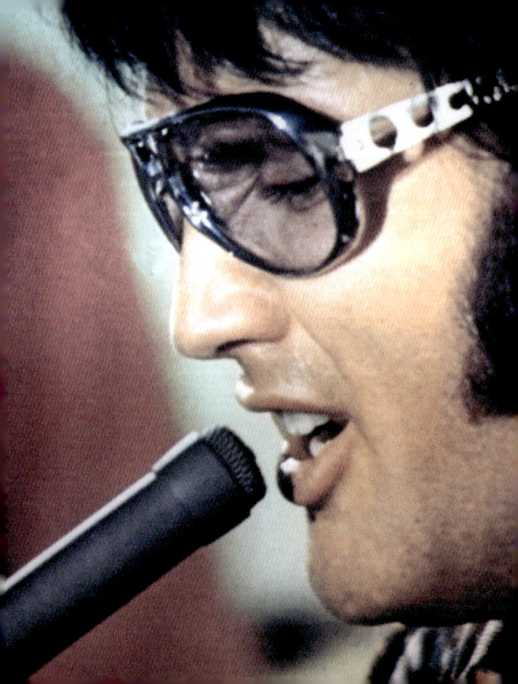

Adversity is sometimes hard upon a man; but for one man who can stand prosperity, there are a hundred that will stand adversity.

—Elvis Presley

Newsweek magazine indirectly credited *Elvis* with creating the idea of the "generation gap." After Elvis appeared on *The Steve Allen Show*, the magazine wrote that "Civilization today is sharply divided into two schools which cannot stand the sight of each other"—parents (who were shocked by his suggestive dancing) and their teenage children (who screamed and swooned at the sight of him).

IS

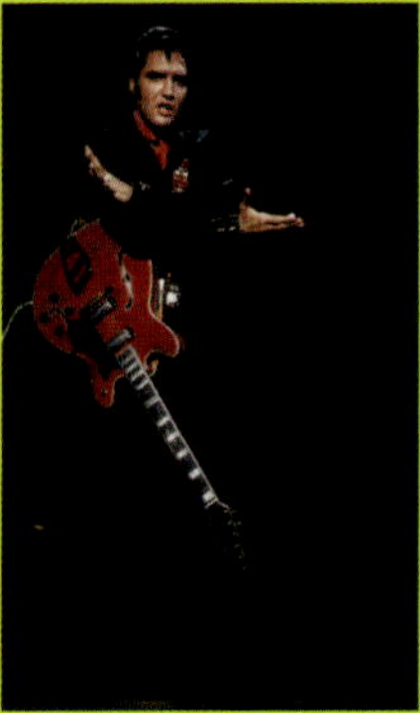

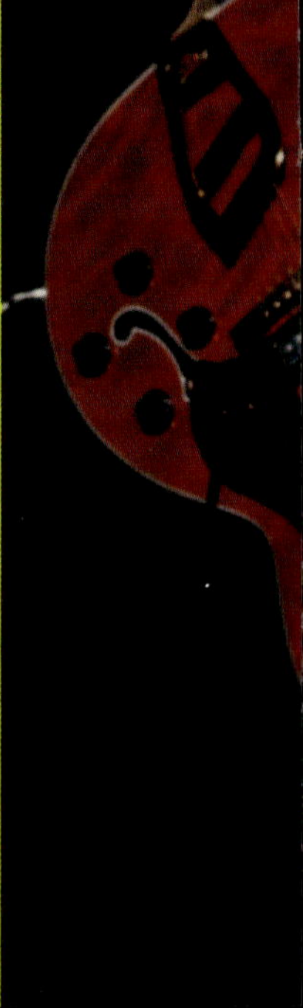

. . . half nervousness, half moving to the beat.

—*Elvis Presley, on his onstage dancing*

When ELVIS

was inducted into the Army, he had to have his famous hair cut off. It was the most photographed haircut in history.

Elvis: The King of Rock 'n' Roll

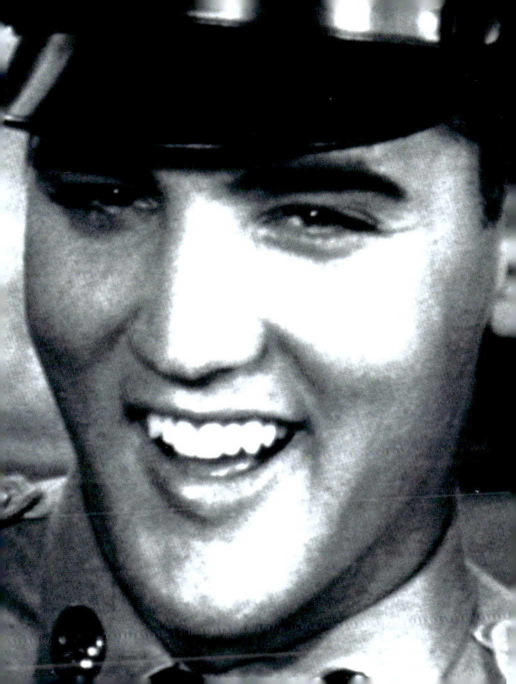

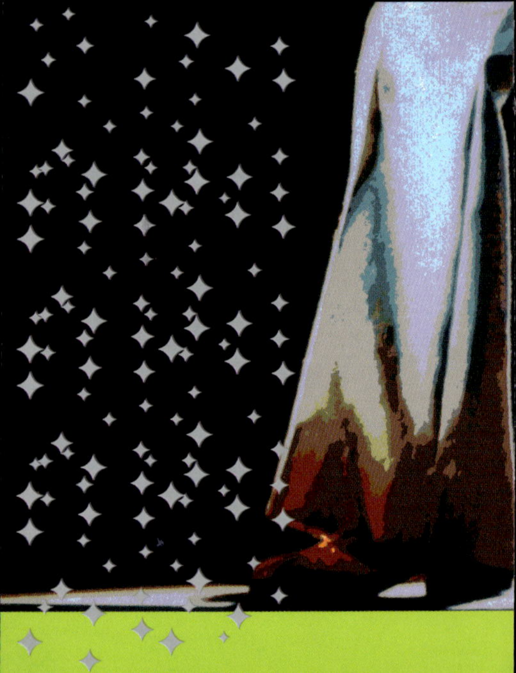

Ambition is a dream with a V8 engine.

—Elvis Presley

Colonel Tom Parker, *Elvis's* shrewd manager, was never a U.S. citizen. Only after *Elvis's* death was it revealed that he was not Thomas Parker from West Virginia, but was Andreas van Kujik from Holland. He was not a colonel either; he'd been given the honorary title by the governor of Tennessee.

Elvis: The King of Rock 'n' Roll

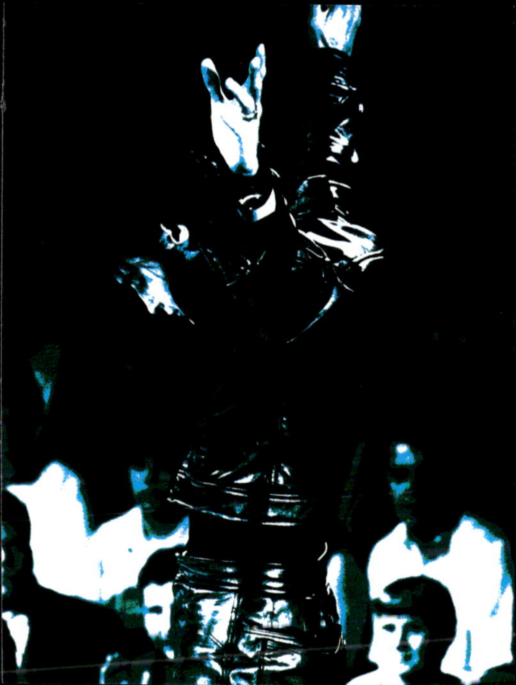

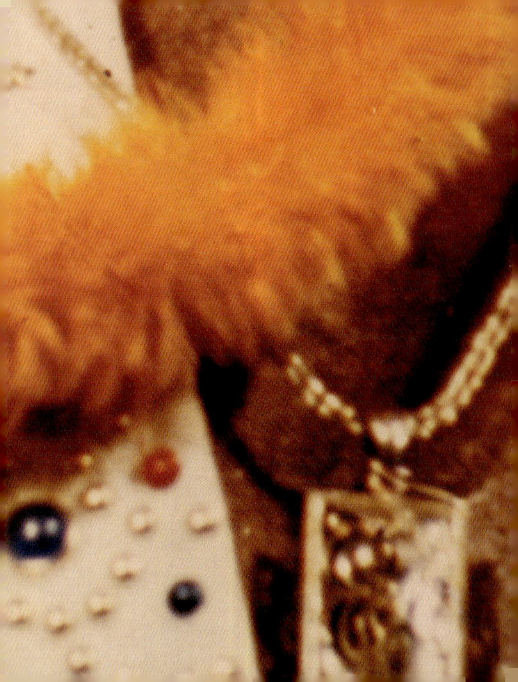

In the 1970s, Elvis took to wearing extravagant outfits covered with rhinestones and other glittering objects, oversized belt buckles, and even floor-length capes. These costumes often weighed as much as thirty pounds.

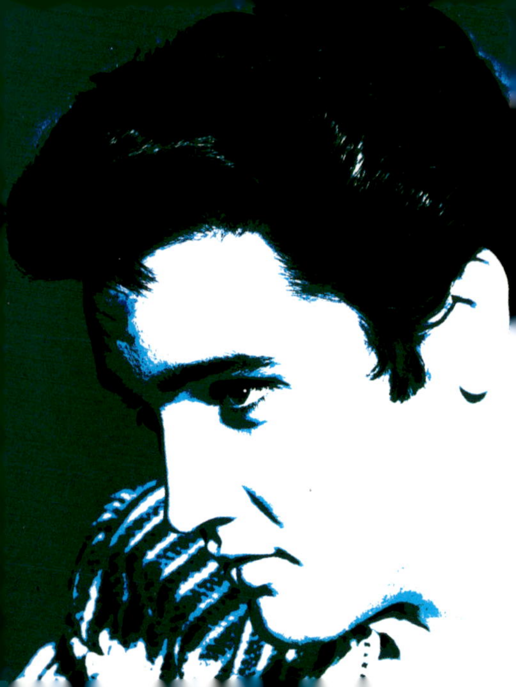

In 1957, *Life* magazine reported that 1,000 girls in Grand Rapids, Michigan, had their hair cut into an *Elvis*-style hairdo.

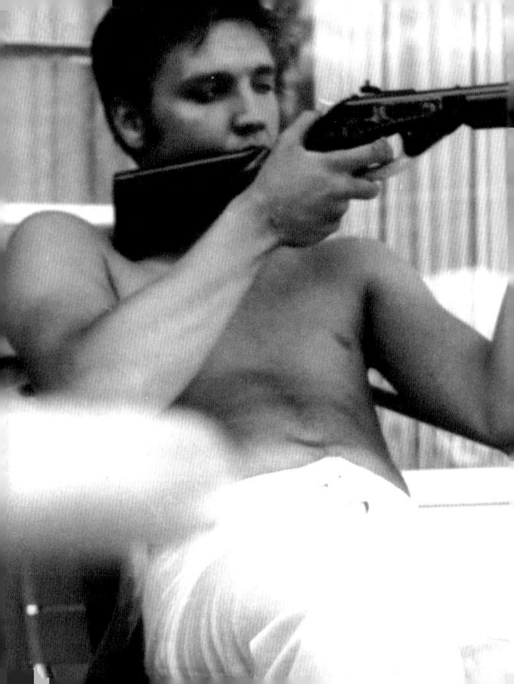

Elvis collected guns but never shot at animals. Instead, he shot a hole through a Graceland TV when a singer he disliked, Robert Goulet, appeared onscreen.

As long as [rock 'n' roll] lasts, I'll continue doing it. As long as that's what the people want. And if they change,

Elvis: The King of Rock 'n' Roll

E L

The King of Rock 'n' Roll